Zany & Brainy

GOOD CLEAN JOKES

for Kids

BOB PHILLIPS

HARVEST HOUSE PUBLISHERS
EUGENE, OREGON

Cover illustration © Leisure Time/Mister Retro

Cover design by Dugan Design Group, Bloomington,
Minnesota

ZANY AND BRAINY GOOD CLEAN JOKES FOR KIDS
Copyright © 2005 by Bob Phillips
Published 2012 by Harvest House Publishers
Eugene, Oregon 97402
www.harvesthousepublishers.com

ISBN 978-0-7369-3072-7 (pbk.)
ISBN 978-0-7369-4295-9 (eBook)

Printed in the United States of America

12 13 14 15 16 17 18 / BP-KB / 10 9 8 7 6 5 4 3 2 1

Contents

1
Crazy Questions

Q: How do you turn a beagle into a bird?
A: Remove the *b*.

Q: How do army frogs march?
A: Hop, two, three, four!

Q: How do eels get out of a muddy seabed?
A: With four-eel drive.

Q: How many hamburgers can you eat on a an empty stomach?
A: Only one, because after that your stomach is no longer empty.

Q: How does a hockey player kiss?
A: He puckers up.

Q: How was your trip to Helsinki?
A: Terrible! All our luggage vanished into Finnair!

Q: How did the inventor discover gunpowder?
A: It came to him in a flash.

Q: How does an artist break up with his girlfriend?
A: He gives her the brush-off.

૭ઢ ૭ઢ ૭ઢ

Q: How can you stop a dog from barking in the backyard?
A: Let him go out front.

૭ઢ ૭ઢ ૭ઢ

Q: How do you catch an electric eel?
A: With a lightning rod.

૭ઢ ૭ઢ ૭ઢ

Q: How many paws does a bear have?
A: One pa and one ma.

૭ઢ ૭ઢ ૭ઢ

Q: How do you fit six elephants in a motorboat?
A: Put three in the front seat and three in the backseat.

Q: How did Robinson Crusoe survive after his boat sank?

A: He used a bar of soap and washed himself ashore.

Ᏸ Ᏸ Ᏸ

Q: How do you make a slow employee fast?

A: Don't give him anything to eat for a while.

2
Theodore & Thaddeus

Theodore: What do joke-book writers eat
for breakfast?
Thaddeus: Search me.
Theodore: Corny flakes.

❧ ❧ ❧

Theodore: What is the best way to paint a
rabbit?
Thaddeus: I'm in the dark.
Theodore: With hare spray.

❧ ❧ ❧

Theodore: What kind of clothes does a house wear?

Thaddeus: I don't have the foggiest.

Theodore: A coat of paint and address.

% % %

Theodore: What would happen if all the goofy people in Chicago jumped into Lake Michigan?

Thaddeus: I'm blank.

Theodore: Lake Michigan would end up with a ring around it.

% % %

Theodore: What type of fish play poker?

Thaddeus: That's a mystery.

Theodore: Card sharks.

% % %

Theodore: What is a fish's favorite game?

Thaddeus: I have no idea.

Theodore: Salmon Says.

% % %

Theodore: What famous inventor loved practical jokes?

Thaddeus: I don't know.

Theodore: Benjamin Pranklin.

℘   ℘   ℘

Theodore: What kind of geese are found in Portugal?

Thaddeus: I pass.

Theodore: Portu-geese.

℘   ℘   ℘

Theodore: What do you take for motion sickness on a cruise?

Thaddeus: Beats me.

Theodore: Vitamin sea.

℘   ℘   ℘

Theodore: What would you get if you blew your hair dryer down a rabbit hole?

Thaddeus: My mind is a blank.

Theodore: Hot, cross bunnies.

℘   ℘   ℘

Theodore: What kind of vehicle does a hog drive?
Thaddeus: Who knows?
Theodore: A pig-up truck.

❦ ❦ ❦

Theodore: What would you get if you crossed an eagle and a skunk?
Thaddeus: I give up.
Theodore: An animal with a high stink.

❦ ❦ ❦

Theodore: What did the bus driver say to the fish?
Thaddeus: You tell me.
Theodore: "What school do you go to?"

❦ ❦ ❦

Theodore: What will not speak unless it is spoken to and cannot be seen but only heard?
Thaddeus: I have no clue.
Theodore: An echo.

ꙮ ꙮ ꙮ

Theodore: What do you say when you want
    to stop a boat?
Thaddeus: I can't guess.
Theodore: "Whoa, whoa, whoa the boat."

ꙮ ꙮ ꙮ

Theodore: What would you get if you
    crossed a kangaroo with a cow?
Thaddeus: I'm in the dark.
Theodore: A kangamoo.

ꙮ ꙮ ꙮ

Theodore: What should you say if you are
    swimming in the ocean and happen to
    get entangled in kelp?
Thaddeus: I don't have the foggiest.
Theodore: "*KELP!*"

ꙮ ꙮ ꙮ

Theodore: What do you call someone who
　　paints flowers?
Thaddeus: I'm blank.
Theodore: A budding artist.

3
Who's There?

Knock, knock.
Who's there?
Watt.
Watt who?
Watt a bad joke.

Knock, knock.
Who's there?
Adolf.
Adolf who?
Adolf ball hit me in the mowf.

Knock, knock.
Who's there?
Ooze.
Ooze who?
Ooze the person in charge around here?

% % %

Knock, knock.
Who's there?
Viola.
Viola who?
Viola sudden you don't remember me?

% % %

Knock, knock.
Who's there?
Wanda.
Wanda who?
Wanda piece of pumpkin pie?

% % %

Knock, knock.
Who's there?
Dick.

Dick who?
Dick 'em up! I told you this was a holdup.

Knock, knock.
Who's there?
Thumping.
Thumping who?
Thumping green and slimy is crawling on
    your shoulder.

Knock, knock.
Who's there?
Rose.
Rose who?
Rows, rows, rows your boat.

Knock, knock.
Who's there?
Value.
Value who?
Value be my valentine? And value please let
    me in?

Knock, knock.
Who's there?
Omar.
Omar who?
Omar goodness gracious! I must have
    knocked on the wrong door.

Knock, knock.
Who's there?
Tibet.
Tibet who?
Tibet you can't guess who's knocking at the
    door.

Knock, knock.
Who's there?
Yule.
Yule who?
Yule know as soon as you open the door.

Knock, knock.
Who's there?
Zippy.
Zippy who?
Mrs. Zippy. Can you spell that without any
    i's?

℘ ℘ ℘

Knock, knock.
Who's there?
Utah Nevada.
Utah Nevada who?
Utah Nevada guess where I went for a
    vacation.

℘ ℘ ℘

4
Agnus & Arnold

Agnus: What is a cow's favorite television show?
Arnold: Search me.
Agnus: "Steer Trek."

෨ ෨ ෨

Agnus: What happened to the woman who covered herself with vanishing cream?
Arnold: I'm in the dark.
Agnus: Nobody knows.

෨ ෨ ෨

Agnus: What do you call a fish with two legs?

Arnold: I don't have the foggiest.

Agnus: A two-knee fish.

Agnus: What is blue, big, and goes around pouting all day?

Arnold: I'm blank.

Agnus: The Incredible Sulk.

Agnus: What does a moose get when he lifts weights?

Arnold: That's a mystery.

Agnus: Moosles.

Agnus: What would happen if pigs had wings and could fly?

Arnold: I don't know.

Agnus: Bacon would go up.

Agnus: What did the police do when they thought Mark stole a watch?
Arnold: I pass.
Agnus: Question Mark.

ఌ ఌ ఌ

Agnus: What did the whale do when his mom made him go to bed early?
Arnold: Beats me.
Agnus: He blubbered.

ఌ ఌ ఌ

Agnus: What is the fastest way to make a mothball?
Arnold: My mind is a blank.
Agnus: Hit it in the mouth.

ఌ ఌ ఌ

Agnus: What does a bee apply after a shower?
Arnold: Who knows?
Agnus: Bee-odorant.

ఌ ఌ ఌ

Agnus: What do you call a cow without any legs?
Arnold: I give up.
Agnus: Ground beef.

ɞ   ɞ   ɞ

Agnus: What is a billow?
Arnold: You tell me.
Agnus: What you sleep on when you have a bad cold.

ɞ   ɞ   ɞ

Agnus: What has webbed feet, fangs, and flies?
Arnold: Search me.
Agnus: Count Quackula.

ɞ   ɞ   ɞ

Agnus: What do you get from a nervous cow?
Arnold: I'm in the dark.
Agnus: A milk shake.

❡ ❡ ❡

Agnus: What has towns without houses,
    rivers and lakes without any water, and
    parks and forests without any trees?
Arnold: I don't have the foggiest.
Agnus: A road map.

❡ ❡ ❡

Agnus: What famous beach do cows go to
    for the holidays?
Arnold: I'm blank.
Agnus: Mooo-ami Beach.

❡ ❡ ❡

Agnus: What doesn't get any wetter no
    matter how hard it rains?
Arnold: That's a mystery.
Agnus: A lake.

Agnus: What do you call a cow that doesn't give milk?
Arnold: I have no idea.
Agnus: A milk dud.

❧ ❧ ❧

Agnus: What would you call a skeleton that wouldn't do any yard work?
Arnold: I don't know.
Agnus: Lazy bones.

5

The Answer Man

Q: Why does your hand get tired after writing with a pencil for a long time?
A: Because the pencil is full of lead.

ೞ   ೞ   ೞ

Q: Why was the crab crabby when he woke up?
A: The sea snore kept him up all night.

ೞ   ೞ   ೞ

Q: Why did Jack and Jill roll down the hill?
A: They got tired of walking.

❡ ❡ ❡

Q: Why is it impossible to have rain for two nights in a row?
A: Because there is a day between.

❡ ❡ ❡

Q: Why did the woman take her computer to a clinic?
A: It had a virus.

❡ ❡ ❡

Q: Why does underwear last longer than all other clothing?
A: Because it's never worn out.

❡ ❡ ❡

Q: Why did the man go off the side of the cliff with his truck?
A: He wanted to test his air brakes.

Q: Why do they call him Sunny?
A: Because he's such a bright boy.

☜ ☜ ☜

Q: Why is the letter *d* like a bad boy?
A: Because they both make Ma mad.

☜ ☜ ☜

Q: Why is no one allowed to touch live wires?
A: It's too shocking.

☜ ☜ ☜

Q: Why do skunks argue all the time?
A: Because they like to raise a stink.

☜ ☜ ☜

Q: Why did the *a, e, i, o,* and *u* get in trouble?
A: They used vowel language.

☜ ☜ ☜

Q: Why did the Boy Scout get so dizzy?
A: He did too many good turns.

% % %

Q: Why did they let the turkey join the band?
A: Because it had the drumsticks.

% % %

Q: Why do hurricanes travel so fast?
A: If they traveled slowly, we would have to call them slow-i-canes.

% % %

Q: Why was the lamb punished?
A: Because it was baaaa-d.

6
Did You Hear?

Jan: Did you hear about the mother who sent a note with her son to school? It read, "Please excuse my son's tardiness."

Jane: What happened?

Jan: She forgot to wake him up and didn't find him till she started making the bed.

🐛 🐛 🐛

Igor: Did you hear about the cat that loved tennis?

Boris: Why's that?

Igor: He had two brothers in the racket.

ஒ ஒ ஒ

Molly: Did you hear about the riot in the
library?
Mack: I'm in the dark.
Molly: Someone found *time bomb* in the dic-
tionary.

ஒ ஒ ஒ

Did you hear? A man who was driving
through the country saw a hitchhiker with
a rope in his hand. On the end of the rope
was a black-and-white cow.

The driver said, "I can take you, but
your cow won't fit into my car."

"That's no problem. She will follow us by
herself," said the hitchhiker.

The hitchhiker got in, and the driver
stepped on the gas and drove 30 miles an
hour. The cow followed behind the car about
50 feet back. The driver sped up to 50 miles
per hour. Somehow the cow was keeping pace
about 30 feet behind the car. The driver
went to 65 miles per hour. He looked in the
rearview mirror and noticed that the cow
was running 10 feet behind his car with her
tongue hanging out of her mouth.

"I'm worried about your cow," said the driver. "Her tongue is hanging out of her mouth to the right."

"Oh, that's okay," replied the hitchhiker. "That means she wants to pass you."

♋ ♋ ♋

Penny: Did you hear about the sword swallower who wanted to put something away for a rainy day?
Jenny: Tell me about it.
Penny: He swallowed an umbrella.

♋ ♋ ♋

Bill: Did you hear about the generation crisis in reverse?
Jill: I'm blank.
Bill: A teenager drove his car into the garage and ran over his father's bicycle.

♋ ♋ ♋

Ben: Did you hear about the porcupine who bumped into a cactus?
Echo: What happened?

Ben: "Is that you, sweetheart?" he asked
    tenderly.

♋ ♋ ♋

Did you hear about the lady who had a
home computer? When she wasn't around,
her young son, Hans, would play with the
keys. He would always play with the keys
after he had eaten something. So he got
peanut butter and jelly and all kinds of
sticky things on the keys.

After a while, the computer could stand
the mess no longer. One day when the lady
turned on the computer, the following message was on the screen: *I won't do any work
for you until you take your dirty Hans off
me!*

♋ ♋ ♋

John: Did you hear about the baby who was
    so ugly that the mother wouldn't push
    the baby carriage?
Leicia: No. What happened?
John: She pulled it.

♋ ♋ ♋

Jef: What did you think of the picture they took of me?

DeeDee: I think that it makes you look five years older.

Jef: Oh well, that will save me from having one taken five years from now.

❧ ❧ ❧

Dean: Did you miss me while I was away?

Martha: Were you away?

❧ ❧ ❧

Brad: Did you hear about the kamikaze pilot who had trouble with indecision?

Liz: My mind is a blank.

Brad: He flew 105 missions.

7
Conroy & Cora

Conroy: What will stay hot the longest in the refrigerator?
Cora: Search me.
Conroy: Red pepper.

    ❧ ❧ ❧

Conroy: What is full of holes but still holds water?
Cora: I'm in the dark.
Conroy: A sponge.

    ❧ ❧ ❧

Conroy: What is red, white, and blue, and
    handy if you sneeze?
Cora: I don't have the foggiest.
Conroy: Hanky Doodle Dandy.

೦౭   ೦౭   ೦౭

Conroy: What happened to the man who
    claimed he ate a 30-foot pizza?
Cora: I'm blank.
Conroy: He had a bitemare!

೦౭   ೦౭   ೦౭

Conroy: What nut is like a sneeze?
Cora: That's a mystery.
Conroy: A cashew.

೦౭   ೦౭   ೦౭

Conroy: What's orange and falls off walls?
Cora: I have no idea.
Conroy: Humpty Pumpkin.

೦౭   ೦౭   ೦౭

Conroy: What telephone number does a pig call when it gets into trouble?
Cora: I don't know.
Conroy: Swine one one.

❧ ❧ ❧

Conroy: What's green, has a red nose, and guides Santa's sleigh?
Cora: I pass.
Conroy: Rudolph the Red-Nosed Pickle.

❧ ❧ ❧

Conroy: What do you get if you cross a cocker spaniel, a poodle, and a rooster?
Cora: Beats me.
Conroy: A cockapoodledoo.

❧ ❧ ❧

Conroy: What do you call it when a bean goes swimming?
Cora: My mind is a blank.
Conroy: A bean dip.

❧ ❧ ❧

Conroy: What do they call a person who looks over your shoulder while you are eating at the lunch counter?
Cora: Who knows?
Conroy: A counterspy.

❧ ❧ ❧

Conroy: What did the cat give the dog for his birthday?
Cora: I give up.
Conroy: Collie-flowers.

❧ ❧ ❧

Conroy: What kind of house weighs the least?
Cora: You tell me.
Conroy: A lighthouse, of course.

❧ ❧ ❧

Conroy: What is the pig's favorite vacation spot?

Cora: I have no clue.
Conroy: Wallow Wallow, Washington.

℘   ℘   ℘

Conroy: What do you do if you have a ring
in your nose?
Cora: I can't guess.
Conroy: You had better answer it.

℘   ℘   ℘

Conroy: What is the fastest way to remove
varnish?
Cora: Search me.
Conroy: Take away the letter *r*.

℘   ℘   ℘

Conroy: What part of a fish weighs the
most?
Cora: I'm in the dark.
Conroy: Its scales.

℘   ℘   ℘

Conroy: What is the easiest way to tell the difference between a hen and a rooster?

Cora: I don't have the foggiest.

Conroy: Toss some corn on the ground. If he eats it, it's a rooster; if she eats it, it's a hen.

8
Teachers

Teacher: Why did the two wrestlers have to fight in the dark?
Student: Because their match wouldn't light.

❧   ❧   ❧

Teacher: Here is a hard question. Name an animal that lives in Lapland.
Student: A reindeer.
Teacher: That's great. Now name another.
Student: Another reindeer.

❧   ❧   ❧

Teacher: What number comes after 4?
Student: All the rest of them.

ॐ ॐ ॐ

Teacher: Who wrote, "Oh, say can you see?"
Student: An eye doctor.

ॐ ॐ ॐ

Teacher: Give me a sentence with the word
fascinate in it.
Student: If I had a sweater with ten but-
tons and two of them fell off, I could
then only fasten eight.

ॐ ॐ ॐ

Teacher: Do you know what they call an
Indian reservation?
Student: The home of the brave.

ॐ ॐ ॐ

Teacher: What's big, purple, and lies across
the sea from us?
Student: Grape Britain.

ॐ ॐ ॐ

Teacher: Give me a sentence starting with *I*.

Student: Okay. "I is..."

Teacher: No, no! You do not say "I is." You say "I am."

Student: Okay. "I am the ninth letter of the alphabet."

ભ ભ ભ

Teacher: What did you do this summer?

Student: This summer I did absolutely nothing all day. Now I know what it's like to be a teacher.

ભ ભ ભ

Teacher: You mustn't fight. You should learn to give and take.

Student: I did. He took my Mars bar, and I gave him a black eye!

ભ ભ ભ

Teacher: I would like you to spell *Tennessee*.

Student: Okay. "One-a-see, two-a-see, three-a-see..."

9

Buddy & Burges

Buddy: What kind of ties can't you wear?
Burges: Search me.
Buddy: Railroad ties.

❧ ❧ ❧

Buddy: What do you call a mummy convention?
Burges: I'm in the dark.
Buddy: A wrap session.

❧ ❧ ❧

Buddy: What kind of toys does a psychiatrist's child play with?
Burges: I don't have the foggiest.
Buddy: Mental blocks.

ର ର ର

Buddy: What did one broom say to the other broom?
Burges: I'm blank.
Buddy: "Have you heard the latest dirt?"

ର ର ର

Buddy: What cord is full of knots that no one can untie?
Burges: That's a mystery.
Buddy: A cord of wood.

ର ର ର

Buddy: What did one shrub say to the other shrub?
Burges: I have no idea.
Buddy: "Am I bushed!"

ର ର ର

Buddy: What do they call a towel that you look at but never use?
Burges: I don't know.
Buddy: A guest towel.

%@ %@ %@

Buddy: What school is especially for soldiers with a bad sense of direction?
Burges: I pass.
Buddy: East Point.

%@ %@ %@

Buddy: What has spots, weighs four tons, and loves peanuts?
Burges: Beats me.
Buddy: An elephant with the measles.

%@ %@ %@

Buddy: What store has the most agreeable salespeople?
Burges: My mind is a blank.
Buddy: Okay-Mart.

Buddy: What did the farmer do when he found that 300 hares escaped from his rabbit farm?
Burges: Who knows?
Buddy: He combed the area.

     ❧   ❧   ❧

Buddy: What kind of jokes does a podia- trist like?
Burges: I give up.
Buddy: Corny jokes.

     ❧   ❧   ❧

Buddy: What is more invisible than the invisible man?
Burges: You tell me.
Buddy: The shadow of the invisible man.

     ❧   ❧   ❧

Buddy: What number can you divide in half and have nothing?
Burges: I have no clue.
Buddy: 8.

෯ ෯ ෯

Buddy: What can you hold in your right hand but not in your left hand?
Burges: I can't guess.
Buddy: Your left elbow.

෯ ෯ ෯

Buddy: What five-letter word has six left when you take two away?
Burges: Search me.
Buddy: *Sixty.*

෯ ෯ ෯

Buddy: What do you call the most unhappy birds in the world?
Burges: I'm in the dark.
Buddy: Bluebirds.

෯ ෯ ෯

Buddy: What dog stands the best chance of winning the heavyweight title?
Burges: I don't have the foggiest.
Buddy: A boxer, of course!

❧ ❧ ❧

Buddy: What swimming stroke do babies use?
Burges: I'm blank.
Buddy: The crawl.

❧ ❧ ❧

Buddy: What is the world's biggest source of grape juice?
Burges: That's a mystery.
Buddy: The Grape Lakes.

10
Friends

Jeff: Who went into the lion's den and came out alive?

Nole: Daniel.

Jeff: You're right. Who went into the tiger's den and came out alive?

Nole: I don't know.

Jeff: The tiger!

Vic: Did you open a sock factory?

Rick: No. My investors developed cold feet.

Moe: Where did the robber eat lunch?
Joe: Burglar King!

❧ ❧ ❧

Kate: I'm so hungry. I can describe my
      stomach in two letters.
Earl: Which two?
Kate: *M-t.*

❧ ❧ ❧

Tex: What is the laziest mountain?
Lex: Mount Everest.

❧ ❧ ❧

Rocky: Look at those two snails fighting.
Ginger: Shouldn't you break them up?
Rocky: Nah. Let them slug it out.

❧ ❧ ❧

Moe: How do you get firewood?
Joe: Axe for it!

ℭ ℭ ℭ

Tabor: I'm going to invent the wheel.
Ella: That should cause a revolution.

ℭ ℭ ℭ

Nick: Let's grill some hamburgers.
Fletcher: How do you grill hamburgers?
Nick: First, you read them their rights.

ℭ ℭ ℭ

Jane: What's a baby turkey called?
Joan: I don't know. What?
Jane: A peeping tom.

ℭ ℭ ℭ

Eve: You remind me of my favorite boxer.
Steve: Frank Bruno?
Eve: No, he's called Fido.

ℭ ℭ ℭ

Todd: I haven't slept in six days.
Blair: Gracious! You must be exhausted.
Todd : I sleep in the nights.

        🌀 🌀 🌀

Ryan: Last night I had the strangest dream.
     I dreamed I was a muffler on a Volks-
     wagen.
Lisa: And then what happened?
Ryan: I woke up exhausted.

        🌀 🌀 🌀

Johnnie: Hey, Mom, how come I'm the big-
     gest kid in the third grade?
Mom: Because you're 19 years old, that's
     why.

        🌀 🌀 🌀

Little Sally: What does your mother do for
     a headache?
Little Sam: She sends me out to play.

        🌀 🌀 🌀

Owen: What do you get if you cross a pig with a rooster?
Clay: You get an animal that goes "oink-a-doodle-doo"!

๑ ๑ ๑

Nate: What is the quickest mountain?
Josh: Mount Rushmore.

๑ ๑ ๑

Ernie: Waiter, there's a fly in my soup!
Waiter: They don't care what they eat, do they, sir?

๑ ๑ ๑

Bert: Waiter, there's a fly in my soup.
Grant: But it looks like it's dead!
Waiter: Yes, it's the heat that kills them.

11
Lynette & Leroy

Lynette: What do they call a dinosaur that goes around wrecking everything?
Leroy: Search me.
Lynette: Tyrannosaurus Wrecks.

ॐ ॐ ॐ

Lynette: What do you call a carpenter who misplaces his tools?
Leroy: I'm in the dark.
Lynette: A saw loser.

ॐ ॐ ॐ

Lynette: What girl has a lot of spare change?
Leroy: I'm blank.
Lynette: Penny!

❧ ❧ ❧

Lynette: What does a duck wear to a fancy party?
Leroy: That's a mystery.
Lynette: A duxedo.

❧ ❧ ❧

Lynette: What kind of ant is good at adding up?
Leroy: I have no idea.
Lynette: An account-ant.

❧ ❧ ❧

Lynette: What is always coming but never arrives?
Leroy: I don't know.
Lynette: Tomorrow.

❧ ❧ ❧

Lynette: What state is the tiniest?
Leroy: I pass.
Lynette: Mini-sota!

❧   ❧   ❧

Lynette: What should you do when your
sister falls asleep in church?
Leroy: Beats me.
Lynette: Poker.

❧   ❧   ❧

Lynette: What do you call a snake that
works for the government?
Leroy: My mind is a blank.
Lynette: A civil serpent.

❧   ❧   ❧

Lynette: What did the tree surgeon say to
the diseased dogwood?
Leroy: Who knows?
Lynette: "Your bark is worse than your
blight."

❧   ❧   ❧

Lynette: What is the difference between
    the North and South Poles?
Leroy: I give up.
Lynette: All the difference in the world.

⚬ ⚬ ⚬

Lynette: What singing grasshopper lives in
    a fireplace?
Leroy: You tell me.
Lynette: Chimney Cricket.

⚬ ⚬ ⚬

Lynette: What do ducks like to watch on
    television?
Leroy: I have no clue.
Lynette: Duckumentaries.

⚬ ⚬ ⚬

Lynette: What shoes should you wear when
    your basement is flooded?
Leroy: I can't guess.
Lynette: Pumps.

⚬ ⚬ ⚬

Lynette: What did George Washington's father do when George cut down the cherry tree?

Leroy: Search me.

Lynette: Flipped his wig.

❦ ❦ ❦

Lynette: What is a thief's favorite game?

Leroy: I'm in the dark.

Lynette: Hide-and-sneak.

❦ ❦ ❦

Lynette: What is the simplest combination of letters?

Leroy: I don't have the foggiest.

Lynette: *E-z.*

❦ ❦ ❦

Lynette: What is the difference between a barber and a woman with many children?

Leroy: I'm blank.

Lynette: One has razors to shave, the other has shavers to raise.

12

Open the Door!

Knock, knock.
Who's there?
Senior.
Senior who?
Senior rubber duckie lately?

Knock, knock.
Who's there?
Aiken.
Aiken who?
Oh, my Aiken back.

Knock, knock.
Who's there?
Yachts.
Yachts who?
Yachts up, Doc?

Knock, knock.
Who's there?
Yah.
Yah who?
Ride 'em, cowboy!

Knock, knock.
Who's there?
Pasture.
Pasture who?
Pasture bedtime, isn't it?

Knock, knock.
Who's there?
Whittle.
Whittle who?
Whittle Orphan Annie.

Knock, knock.
Who's there?
Avenue.
Avenue who?
Avenue heard this knock-knock joke
    before?

Knock, knock.
Who's there?
Just Diane.
Just Diane who?
Just Diane to see you.

Knock, knock.
Who's there?
Amaryllis.
Amaryllis who?
Amaryllis state agent. Wanna buy a house?

Knock, knock.
Who's there?
Dewey.
Dewey who?
Dewey have to listen to all this knocking?

Knock, knock.
Who's there?
Pasta.
Pasta who?
Pasta gravy, please.

Knock, knock.
Who's there?
Jupiter.
Jupiter who?
Jupiter fly in my soup?

Knock, knock.
Who's there?
Wooden.

Wooden who?
Wooden you like to go out with me?

Knock, knock.
Who's there?
Allacin.
Allacin who?
Allacin Wonderland.

Knock, knock.
Who's there?
Kleenex.
Kleenex who?
Kleenex are prettier than dirty necks.

Knock, knock.
Who's there?
Max.
Max who?
Max no difference. Let me in.

13
Elvira & Elvis

Elvira: What animal is satisfied with the
    least nourishment?
Elvis: Search me.
Elvira: Moths. They eat nothing but holes.

ೂ   ೂ   ೂ

Elvira: What was the dog doing in the mud
    puddle?
Elvis: I'm in the dark.
Elvira: Making mutt pies.

ೂ   ೂ   ೂ

Elvira: What do you call a sheep that visits
    a lion on his vacation?

Elvis: I don't have the foggiest.
Elvira: Dinner.

๙ ๙ ๙

Elvira: What is the fastest way to get rich
by eating?
Elvis: That's a mystery.
Elvira: Eat fortune cookies.

๙ ๙ ๙

Elvira: What foods stick together?
Elvis: I have no idea.
Elvira: Staple foods.

๙ ๙ ๙

Elvira: What did one big toe say to the
other big toe?
Elvis: I don't know.
Elvira: "Don't look now, but there's a couple
of big heels following us."

๙ ๙ ๙

Elvira: What is the fastest fish in the water?
Elvis: I pass.
Elvira: Motor-pike.

ᘒ   ᘒ   ᘒ

Elvira: What do you feed your pet frog?
Elvis: Beats me.
Elvira: Croakers and milk!

ᘒ   ᘒ   ᘒ

Elvira: What sea creature will not do any-
thing without a good reason?
Elvis: My mind is a blank.
Elvira: A porpoise.

ᘒ   ᘒ   ᘒ

Elvira: What kind of girl does a hamburger
like?
Elvis: Who knows?
Elvira: Any girl named Patty.

ᘒ   ᘒ   ᘒ

Elvira: What does a frog say when it sees
something great?
Elvis: You tell me.
Elvira: "Toadly awesome!"

ᘒ   ᘒ   ᘒ

Elvira: What do you get if you cross a cat
    and a lemon?
Elvis: I have no clue.
Elvira: A sourpuss.

           ᗱ   ᗱ   ᗱ

Elvira: What do you get when you cross a
    trumpet and a flute?
Elvis: Search me.
Elvira: A tootie-flooty.

           ᗱ   ᗱ   ᗱ

Elvira: What do you get when you cross a
    horse and a cow?
Elvis: I don't have the foggiest.
Elvira: Whinny the Moo.

14
Tongue Twisters

The back black brake block box broke badly.

Betty Bliss blended blue-black blueberries
in the blender.

He says she says she shall sew satin sheets
shut.

Just Judge Jerry Jennings judges justly.

Sally saves six Swiss wrist Swatch watches.

Selfish Sheriff Sam Short should share
some shellfish.

The sharp shark shop sells short silk shorts.

Should she shun such silly subjects?

Sixty sleepy sheep shun sunshine shearing.

Sulky Sascha slightly sews slashed sheets
slowly.

Surely the soft summer sun shall shine
soon.

Three free figs float freely.

15

Questions & Answers

Q: Why did the rabbit cross the road?
A: To get to the hopping mall.

Q: Why do birds fly south for the winter?
A: Because it's too far to walk.

Q: Why didn't the elephant cross the road?
A: It didn't want to be mistaken for a chicken.

ᘐ ᘐ ᘐ

Q: Why did the paintbrush retire?
A: It had a stroke.

ᘐ ᘐ ᘐ

Q: Why did the turtle cross the road?
A: To get to the shell station.

ᘐ ᘐ ᘐ

Q: Why did the comedian's wife sue for divorce?
A: She claimed he was trying to joke her to death.

ᘐ ᘐ ᘐ

Q: Why did the chopped meat get slapped in the face?
A: It was fresh!

Q: Why did the traffic light turn red?
A: If you had to change in front of all those people, you would turn red, too.

๛   ๛   ๛

Q: Why didn't the elephant cross the street?
A: Because it saw the zebra crossing.

๛   ๛   ๛

Q: Why do lions roar?
A: They would feel silly saying, "Oink, oink."

๛   ๛   ๛

Q: Why can't you tease egg whites?
A: They can't take a yolk!

๛   ๛   ๛

Q: Why do golfers wear two pairs of pants?
A: In case they get a hole in one.

๛   ๛   ๛

Q: Why did the chicken cross the road?
A: To see a man lay bricks.

❧ ❧ ❧

Q: Why did the girl put on a wet dress?
A: Because the label said "wash and wear."

❧ ❧ ❧

Q: Why did the umpire throw the chicken out of the baseball game?
A: He suspected fowl play.

❧ ❧ ❧

Q: Why do your friends carry the letter r around with them?
A: Because without it, your friends would become fiends.

❧ ❧ ❧

Q: Why is a sleeping baby like a hijacking?
A: Because it's a kid napping.

16
Carina & Carlos

Carina: What is the name of the famous cartoon maker who lived in a safe?
Carlos: Search me.
Carina: Vault Disney.

ᘍ ᘍ ᘍ

Carina: What kind of toy does the Godfather play with in the tub?
Carlos: I'm in the dark.
Carina: A thug-boat.

ᘍ ᘍ ᘍ

Carina: What movie channel should you
watch with a can of air freshener
handy?
Carlos: I don't have the foggiest.
Carina: H-BO.

❧   ❧   ❧

Carina: What do you call a blind buck?
Carlos: I'm blank.
Carina: I have no-eye-deer either.

❧   ❧   ❧

Carina: What would happen to Ray if he
were to jump off the Brooklyn Bridge?
Carlos: That's a mystery.
Carina: They would call him X-Ray.

❧   ❧   ❧

Carina: What should you say when you meet
a person with two heads?
Carlos: I don't know.
Carina: Hello, hello!

❧   ❧   ❧

Carina: What do you call a robot that always takes the longest route?
Carlos: I pass.
Carina: R2 Detour.

%% %% %%

Carina: What would be the best thing to do if you found you had water on the knee, water on the elbow, and water on the brain?
Carlos: Beats me.
Carina: Turn off the shower.

%% %% %%

Carina: What do you call a woman who taps telephones?
Carlos: My mind is a blank.
Carina: A lady bug.

%% %% %%

Carina: What do they call someone who thinks he can fly by flapping his arms?
Carlos: Who knows?
Carina: Plane crazy.

Carina: What did the owl do when his owner
    abandoned him?
Carlos: I give up.
Carina: Nothing. He didn't give a hoot.

Carina: What is the best thing to put angel
    food cake into?
Carlos: You tell me.
Carina: Your teeth.

Carina: What do you call a bird gangster?
Carlos: I have no clue.
Carina: Robin Hood.

Carina: What do they call a very selfish
    girl?
Carlos: I can't guess.
Carina: Mimi.

❧ ❧ ❧

Carina: What happens when an insect talks
    too much?
Carlos: Search me.
Carina: It becomes a hoarse fly.

❧ ❧ ❧

Carina: What is the best way to file a knife?
Carlos: I'm in the dark.
Carina: Under the letter k.

❧ ❧ ❧

Carina: What goes "oink-oink" and steals
    your money?
Carlos: I don't have the foggiest.
Carina: A pig-pocket.

❧ ❧ ❧

Carina: What do you get if you cross a skunk
    with a boomerang?
Carlos: I'm blank.
Carina: A terrible smell you can't get rid of.

❦ ❦ ❦

Carina: What should you do if you find a tiger in your bed?
Carlos: That's a mystery.
Carina: Sleep somewhere else!

17
What If?

Q: If there are 17 boys and only 6 apples, what is the easiest way to equally divide the apples among the boys?
A: Make applesauce.

❧ ❧ ❧

Q: If a telegraph operator from New Mexico married a telephone operator from Nevada, what would they become?
A: A Western Union.

❧ ❧ ❧

Q: If you were swimming in the ocean and a big alligator attacked you, what should you do?

A: Nothing. There are no alligators in the ocean.

ೢ ೢ ೢ

Q: If a band were playing music during a lightning storm, who would be in the most danger of being struck by lightning?

A: The conductor.

ೢ ೢ ೢ

Q: If the green house is on the north, the red house on the south, and the purple house on the east, where is the White House?

A: In Washington, D.C.

ೢ ೢ ೢ

Q: If you were invited out to dinner and saw nothing but a beet on your plate, what would you say?

A: That beet's all!

❧ ❧ ❧

Q: If a horse is tied to a 20-foot rope, how can it reach a pile of hay that is 40 feet away?
A: The rope is not tied to anything.

❧ ❧ ❧

Q: If a man were born in Russia, raised in Brazil, came to America, and died in Dallas, Texas, what is he?
A: Dead.

❧ ❧ ❧

Q: If King Kong went to Hong Kong to play Ping-Pong and he died, what would they put on his coffin?
A: A lid.

❧ ❧ ❧

Q: If you crossed a frog and a rabbit, what would you get?
A: A bunny ribbit.

❧ ❧ ❧

Q: If an African lion fought an African tiger, which one do you think would win?

A: Neither one. There are no tigers in Africa.

18

Gwendolyn & Godfrey

Gwendolyn: What is the best way to pass a geometry test?
Godfrey: Search me.
Gwendolyn: Know all the angles.

ॐ ॐ ॐ

Gwendolyn: What happened to the man who took a 100-foot dive into a glass of root beer?
Godfrey: I'm in the dark.
Gwendolyn: Nothing. It was a soft drink.

ॐ ॐ ॐ

Gwendolyn: What do you call a cat that falls into a trash can?

Godfrey: I don't have the foggiest.

Gwendolyn: Kitty litter.

ॐ ॐ ॐ

Gwendolyn: What type of airplane does the pope like to fly in?

Godfrey: I'm blank.

Gwendolyn: A holy-copter.

ॐ ॐ ॐ

Gwendolyn: What did the dirt say to the rain?

Godfrey: That's a mystery.

Gwendolyn: "If this keeps up, my name will be mud."

ॐ ॐ ॐ

Gwendolyn: What message is recorded the same whether it is from right to left or up and down?

Godfrey: I have no idea.

Gwendolyn: SOS.

❧ ❧ ❧

Gwendolyn: What happened when the pig
    couldn't get up from his fall?
Godfrey: I don't know.
Gwendolyn: He called a ham-bulance.

❧ ❧ ❧

Gwendolyn: What kind of table has no legs?
Godfrey: I pass.
Gwendolyn: A multiplication table.

❧ ❧ ❧

Gwendolyn: What do you call a bird that's
    been eaten by a cat?
Godfrey: Beats me.
Gwendolyn: A swallow.

❧ ❧ ❧

Gwendolyn: What is a bacteria?
Godfrey: My mind is a blank.
Gwendolyn: The rear entrance of a cafe-
    teria.

❧ ❧ ❧

Gwendolyn: What do sharks eat at barbe-
cues?
Godfrey: Who knows?
Gwendolyn: Clamburgers.

❧ ❧ ❧

Gwendolyn: What is the science of shopping
called?
Godfrey: I give up.
Gwendolyn: Buyology.

❧ ❧ ❧

Gwendolyn: What game do hogs play?
Godfrey: You tell me.
Gwendolyn: Pig-Pong.

❧ ❧ ❧

Gwendolyn: What did Adam say to Eve on
December 24?
Godfrey: I have no clue.
Gwendolyn: "It's Christmas Eve."

❧   ❧   ❧

Gwendolyn: What can you give a bald man
    that he will never part with?
Godfrey: I can't guess.
Gwendolyn: A comb.

❧   ❧   ❧

Gwendolyn: What do they call a lazy rooster?
Godfrey: Search me.
Gwendolyn: A cockle-doodle don't.

❧   ❧   ❧

Gwendolyn: What is the best kind of fish to
    eat with peanut butter?
Godfrey: I'm in the dark.
Gwendolyn: Jellyfish.

❧   ❧   ❧

Gwendolyn: What has one foot on each side
    and one foot in the middle?
Godfrey: I don't have the foggiest.
Gwendolyn: A yardstick.

❧ ❧ ❧

Gwendolyn: What group plays snappy music?
Godfrey: I'm blank.
Gwendolyn: A rubber band.

❧ ❧ ❧

Gwendolyn: What has large antlers and
    frightens cats?
Godfrey: That's a mystery.
Gwendolyn: Mickey Moose.

19
School

Student 1: I don't think my wood shop
    teacher likes me much.
Student 2: What makes you think that?
Student 1: He's teaching me to make a
    coffin.

Teacher: Why was the period between A.D.
    500 and A.D. 1000 known as the Dark
    Ages?
Student: Because those were the days of
    the knights.

Teacher: If you add 79,312 and 46,920, then divide the answer by 39 and multiply by 78, what would you get?
Student: The wrong answer.

❧ ❧ ❧

Teacher: Where are the Andes, Debby?
Student: At the end of the armies, ma'am.

❧ ❧ ❧

Teacher: What's your name? I haven't seen you before.
Student: Richard J. Hanson.
Teacher: Say "sir" when you address me!
Student: All right. Sir Richard J. Hanson.

❧ ❧ ❧

Teacher: If I had 50 apples in my right hand and 30 apples in my left hand, what would I have?
Student: Big hands.

❧ ❧ ❧

Teacher: If your father borrows thirty dollars from me and pays me back at two dollars a month for seven months, how much will he owe me at that time?

Student: Thirty dollars.

Teacher: It doesn't seem like you know much about math.

Student: It doesn't seem like you know much about my father.

% % %

Teacher: Is Latin a dead language?

Student: As dead as dead can be. It killed off all the Romans, and now it's killing me.

% % %

Teacher: Will you please spell *banana* for me.

Student: I don't believe I can.

Teacher: Why not?

Student: Well, I know how to start, but I don't know when to stop.

% % %

Teacher: Education is wonderful!
Student: What do you mean?
Teacher: It helps you worry about things
    all over the world.

ॐ   ॐ   ॐ

Teacher: What is a leading cause of dry
    skin?
Student: Towels.

20
Fredia & Fonzie

Fredia: What do chickens do when they're
    in love?
Fonzie: Search me.
Fredia: They give each other pecks.

🍥   🍥   🍥

Fredia: What do you call it when you use
    someone else's telephone?
Fonzie: I'm in the dark.
Fredia: Free speech.

🍥   🍥   🍥

Fredia: What do you call a carrot that insults a farmer?
Fonzie: I don't have the foggiest.
Fredia: A fresh vegetable.

༝ ༝ ༝

Fredia: What do trees watch on television?
Fonzie: I'm blank.
Fredia: Their favorite sap operas.

༝ ༝ ༝

Fredia: What do you call a bread slice that's been struck by lightning?
Fonzie: That's a mystery.
Fredia: The toast of the town.

༝ ༝ ༝

Fredia: What happens when the human body is completely submerged in water?
Fonzie: I have no idea.
Fredia: The telephone rings.

༝ ༝ ༝

Fredia: What day does a fish hate the most?
Fonzie: I don't know.
Fredia: Fryday.

      ❧   ❧   ❧

Fredia: What is the best way to run over an
      elephant?
Fonzie: Beats me.
Fredia: Climb up its tail, make a mad dash
      to its head, and then slide down its
      trunk to the ground.

      ❧   ❧   ❧

Fredia: What was the snail doing on the
      freeway?
Fonzie: My mind is a blank.
Fredia: About one mile a day.

      ❧   ❧   ❧

Fredia: What do people from the South
      usually drink water out of?
Fonzie: Who knows?
Fredia: Dixie cups.

      ❧   ❧   ❧

Fredia: What man in armor comes down the
    chimney on December 24?
Fonzie: I give up.
Fredia: The knight before Christmas.

       ও   ও   ও

Fredia: What cracks jokes all the time and
    is covered with feathers?
Fonzie: You tell me.
Fredia: A comedi-hen.

       ও   ও   ও

Fredia: What did one eye say to the other
    eye?
Fonzie: I have no clue.
Fredia: Just between you and me, there's
    something that smells.

       ও   ও   ও

Fredia: What has no length, width, or thick-
    ness, but still can be measured?
Fonzie: I can't guess.
Fredia: The temperature.

       ও   ও   ও

Fredia: What did the chimpanzee say when he heard that his sister was going to have a baby?
Fonzie: Search me.
Fredia: "I'll be a monkey's uncle."

❧ ❧ ❧

Fredia: What was Samuel Clemens's pen name?
Fonzie: I didn't know he had a name for his pen.

❧ ❧ ❧

Fredia: What do you call a person who eats too much melon and gets sick?
Fonzie: I don't have the foggiest.
Fredia: A melon-colic.

❧ ❧ ❧

Fredia: What goes "thump, thump, thump, slosh"?
Fonzie: I'm blank.
Fredia: An elephant with one wet sneaker.

21
Where, Oh Where?

Q: Where is Timbuktu?
A: Between Timbuk-one and Timbuk-three.

🍥 🍥 🍥

Q: Where were chickens first fried?
A: In Greece.

🍥 🍥 🍥

Q: Where does a mother octopus shop for clothes for its children?
A: Squids 'R' Us.

Q: Where do chickens dance?
A: At the fowl ball.

Q: Where do fish wash up?
A: In the bass-tub.

Q: Where does Superman get the food he needs to make him strong?
A: At the supermarket.

Q: Where do rabbits go after they get married?
A: On a bunnymoon.

Q: Where do they send homeless dogs?
A: To an arf-anage.

% % %

Q: Where do dishonest people go to read?
A: The lie-brary.

% % %

Q: Where do you buy laundry detergent?
A: In a soapermarket.

% % %

Q: Where do you throw apple cores after
   you've eaten the apple?
A: In a used core lot.

% % %

Q: Where can you find the finest base-
   ment?
A: On the best-cellar list.

% % %

Q: Where does a pickle love to eat?
A: In a dilly-catessen.

❧ ❧ ❧

Q: Where is the best place to have a broken bone?
A: On someone else.

❧ ❧ ❧

Q: Where did the fish go on vacation?
A: Finland.

❧ ❧ ❧

Q: Where do you find tigers?
A: It depends on where you leave them.

❧ ❧ ❧

Q: Where was the Declaration of Independence signed?
A: At the bottom.

❧ ❧ ❧

Q: Where do bacteria go on vacation?
A: Germany.

❀ ❀ ❀

Q: Where did the cowboy go on his vacation?
A: To Gallup, New Mexico.

❀ ❀ ❀

Q: Where do fish go to get a degree?
A: To tuna-versities.

❀ ❀ ❀

Q: Where do elderly eggs live?
A: In an old yolks home.

❀ ❀ ❀

Q: Where do you put your dog when you go
shopping?
A: In the barking lot.

❀ ❀ ❀

Q: Where did Santa Claus go on his vacation?
A: To a ho-ho-ho-tel.

ও   ও   ও

Q: Where do you take sick kangaroos?
A: To the hop-ital.

22

More Friends

Alisa: Can you tell me the joke about the broken pencil?
Matt: No.
Alisa: Why not?
Matt: It doesn't have any point.

❧ ❧ ❧

Darlene: I have a bad head cold. How can I prevent it from reaching my chest?
Jefrey: Tie a knot in your neck.

❧ ❧ ❧

Ben: There are 15 reasons why I'm not at
the top of my class.
Arnold: What are they?
Ben: The other kids in my class.

❧   ❧   ❧

Paula: What wobbles when it flies?
Jack: A jelly-copter.

❧   ❧   ❧

Tim: Where did your mom go on vacation?
Jim: Alaska.
Tim: Never mind. I'll ask her myself!

❧   ❧   ❧

Mary: Who takes after his father?
Larry: A thief's son.

❧   ❧   ❧

Willy: What happens when you play a country
song backward?
Billy: You get your dog back, your truck
back, and your girlfriend back!

❧ ❧ ❧

Ted: What is a frog's favorite soft drink?
Tad: Croak-a-Cola!

❧ ❧ ❧

Bertie: Who are most of the fish in the
    ocean afraid of?
Gertie: Search me.
Bertie: Jack the Kipper.

❧ ❧ ❧

Jack: What dog swims underwater?
Mac: Scuba Doo.

❧ ❧ ❧

Gail: Why did the elephant cross the road?
Dale: To visit the chicken.

❧ ❧ ❧

Jan: Who invented spaghetti?
Bud: It must have been someone who used
    his noodle.

Jarred: What's a bee's favorite fruit?
Kaylee: A bee-nana.

Glen: What is the dumbest state?
Jen: Flori-duh.

Flip: What did King Kong say when his sister had a baby?
Flop: My mind is blank.
Flip: "Well, I'll be a monkey's uncle."

Jerry: Did you hear the joke about the scissors?
Larry: Yeah, shear nonsense!

Fran: What do you like best about bakery school?
Ann: Roll call.

୧ ୧ ୧

Bonnie: Who can stay single even if he marries many women?
Johnnie: A minister.

୧ ୧ ୧

Jane: If you want to spread gossip, what should you do?
Lane: Tell-a-phone.

୧ ୧ ୧

Ed: Did you buy that new milk store?
Fred: No. The deal went sour.

୧ ୧ ୧

Gideon: Who does Clark Kent turn into when he is hungry?
Gloria: Beats me.
Gideon: Supperman.

୧ ୧ ୧

Lou: What did the cow say on January 1?
Sue: "Happy Moo Year!"